EYE TRICKS

Published and distributed by
TOBAR LIMITED
The Old Aerodrome, Worlingham, Beccles,
Suffolk, NR34 7SP, UK
www.tobar.co.uk

This edition printed in 2009

© 2003 Arcturus Publishing Limited

Printed in China

ISBN: 978 1 903230 11 4

All of the Images contained throughout the Work were created by and are the copyright of the Author, Gary W. Priester, who lives in Placitas, New Mexico USA and can be contacted via e-mail at gary@gwpriester.com.

eyetricks.com

TIPS FOR VIEWING 3D STEREOGRAMS

Stereograms are 3D images hidden within another picture, but they can often be difficult to see. Follow these tips and keep trying – you'll soon get the hang of it.

• Bring the image up close to your face *without* attempting to focus. Slowly move away from the image and keep your eyes relaxed. Before you reach arms length, a picture should jump out at you.

• Hold the image about arm's length in front of you but focus on something behind it. Shift your field of vision to the image without shifting focus. The image should be apparent if your focus is correct.

• Put reflective glass in front of the image and focus on your reflection. At the proper distance, this should allow you to see the 3D object.

Some people see the 3D picture very quickly, others may need to spend awhile practicing before seeing their first stereogram. Still others never see the image. If you are having difficulties, remember to be patient. If you know of someone who can see the images, ask for advice. There are a lot of different tricks people use to see the images.

Seeing the 3D object for the first time can be surprising. You don't expect to see something stand out from the page.

Good luck!

Eye Tricks

VIEW THIS WAY

Eye Tricks

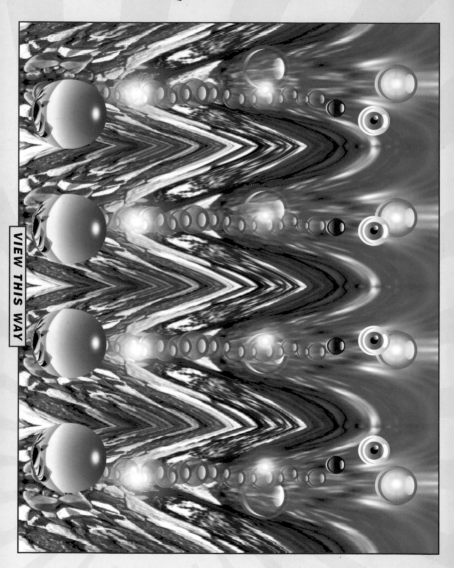

VIEW THIS WAY

Eye Tricks

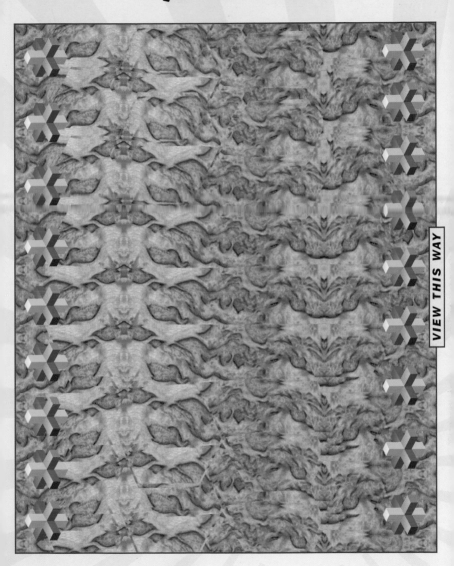

VIEW THIS WAY

Eye Tricks

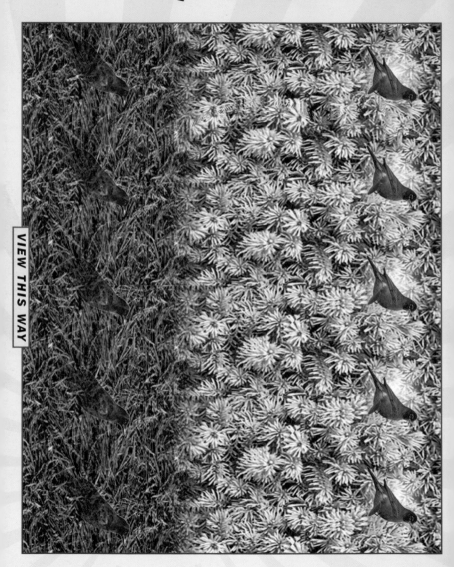

VIEW THIS WAY

Eye Tricks

VIEW THIS WAY

Eye Tricks

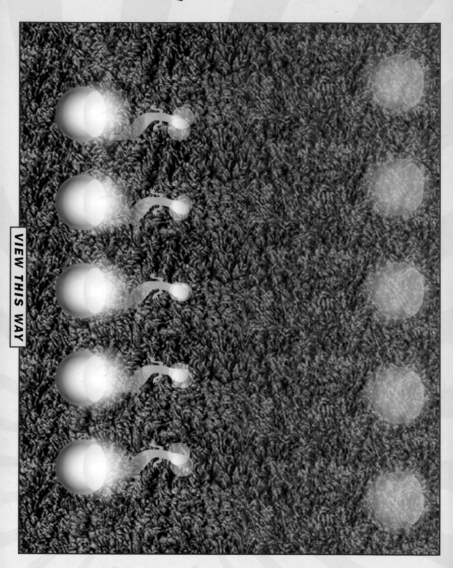

Eye Tricks

VIEW THIS WAY

VIEW THIS WAY

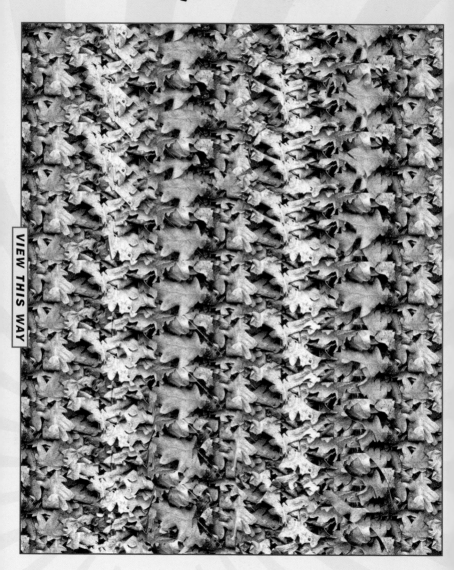

Eye Tricks

VIEW THIS WAY

Eye Tricks

VIEW THIS WAY

14

Eye Tricks

VIEW THIS WAY

Eye Tricks

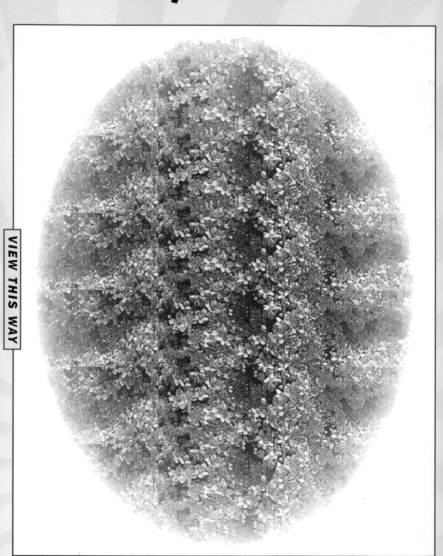

Eye Tricks

VIEW THIS WAY

Eye Tricks

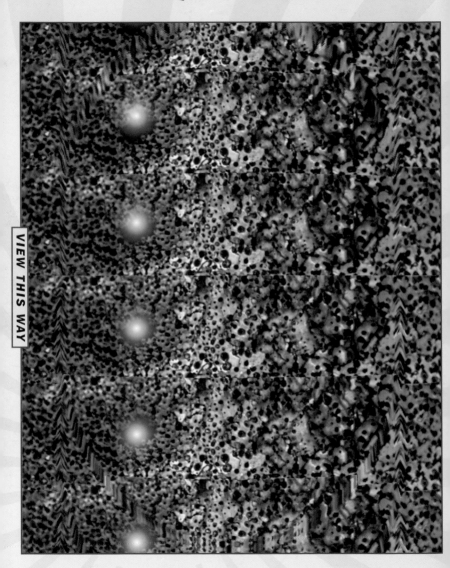

VIEW THIS WAY

Eye Tricks

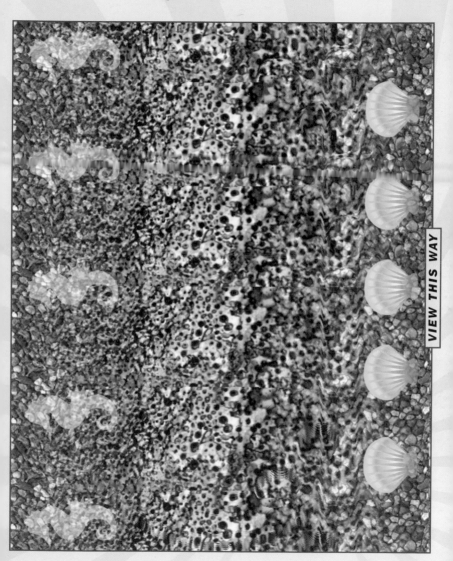

VIEW THIS WAY

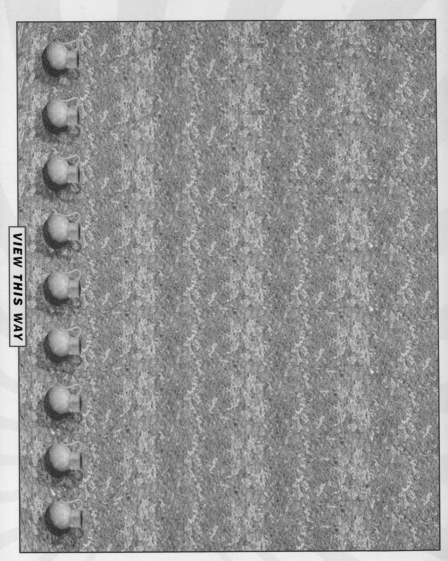

VIEW THIS WAY

Eye Tricks

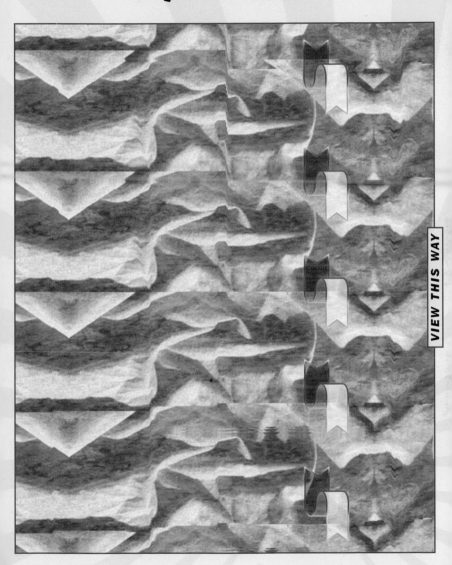

VIEW THIS WAY

21

Eye Tricks

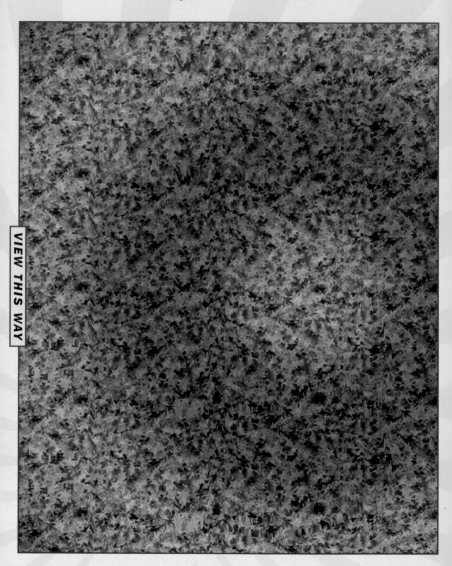

VIEW THIS WAY

22

Eye Tricks

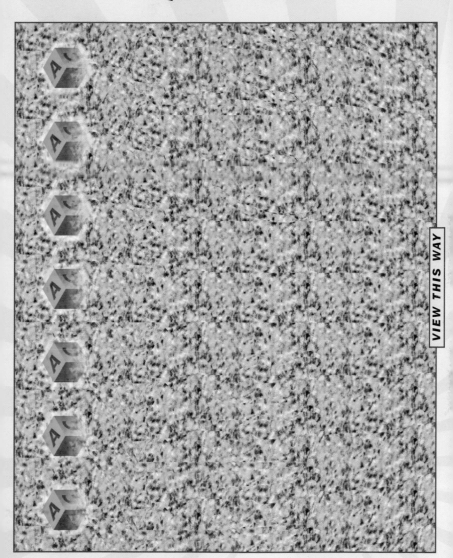

VIEW THIS WAY

23

CELADON

VIEW THIS WAY

Eye Tricks

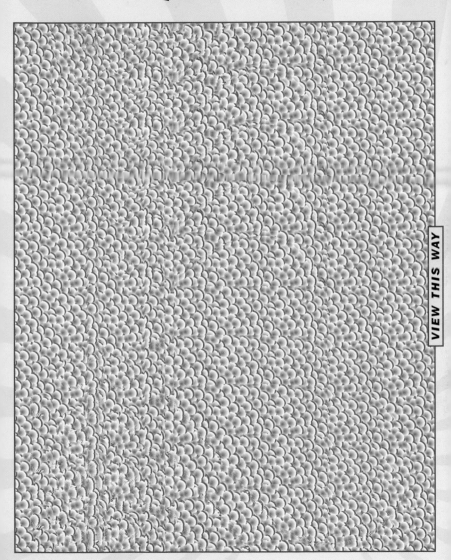

VIEW THIS WAY

Eye Tricks

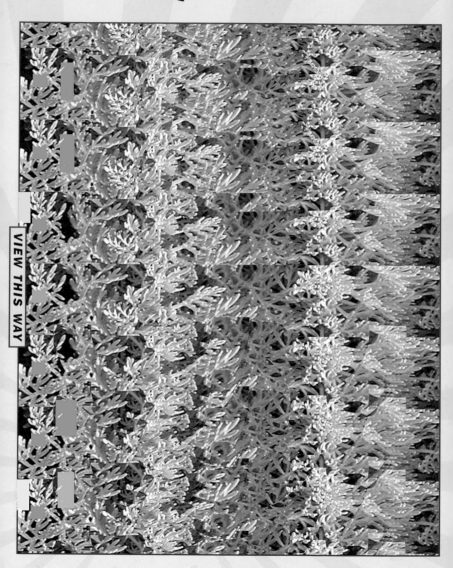

Eye Tricks

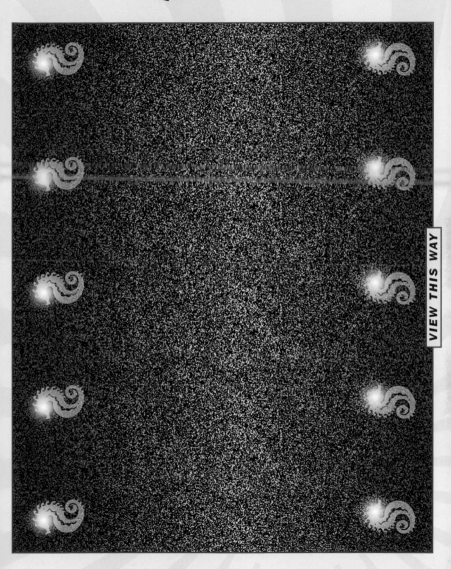

VIEW THIS WAY

Eye Tricks

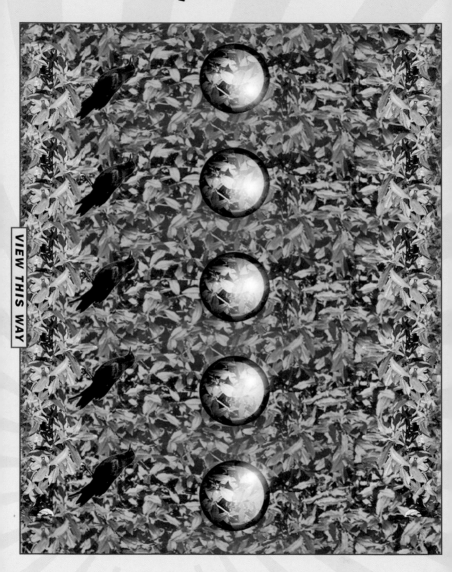

Eye Tricks

VIEW THIS WAY

29

Eye Tricks

VIEW THIS WAY

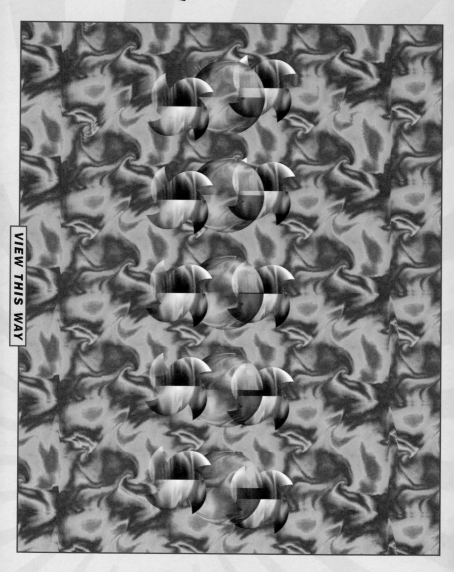

30

Eye Tricks

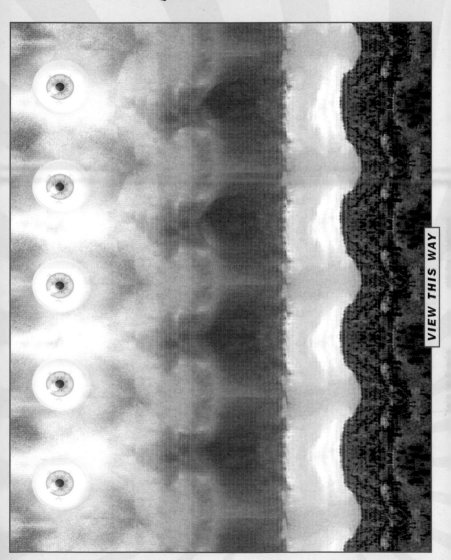

VIEW THIS WAY

Eye Tricks

VIEW THIS WAY

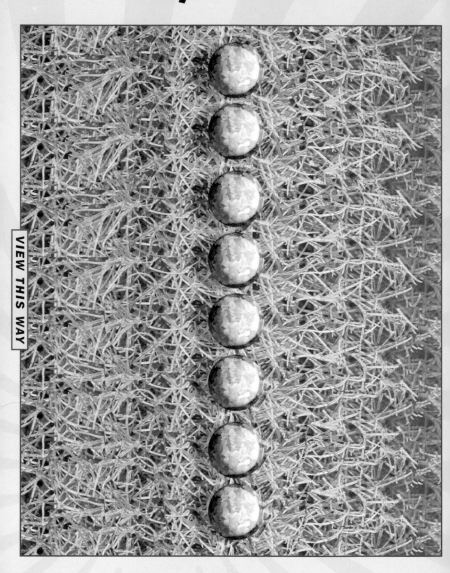

Eye Tricks

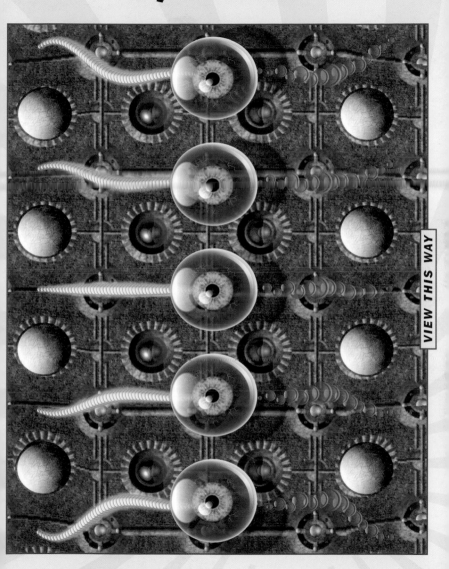

VIEW THIS WAY

Eye Tricks

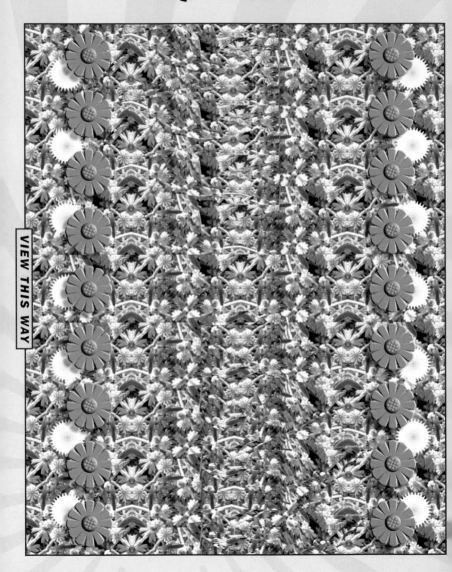

VIEW THIS WAY

Eye Tricks

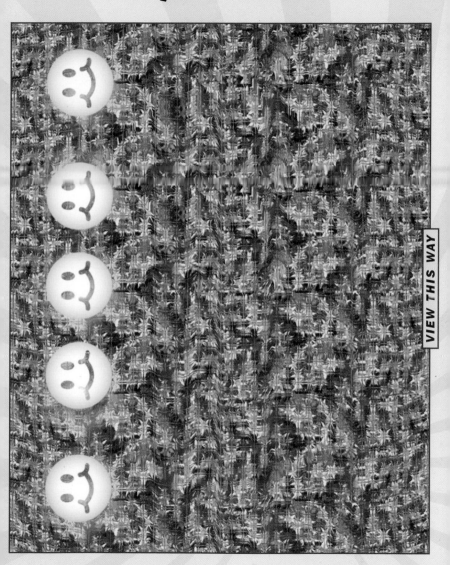

35

Eye Tricks

VIEW THIS WAY

Eye Tricks

VIEW THIS WAY

37

Eye Tricks

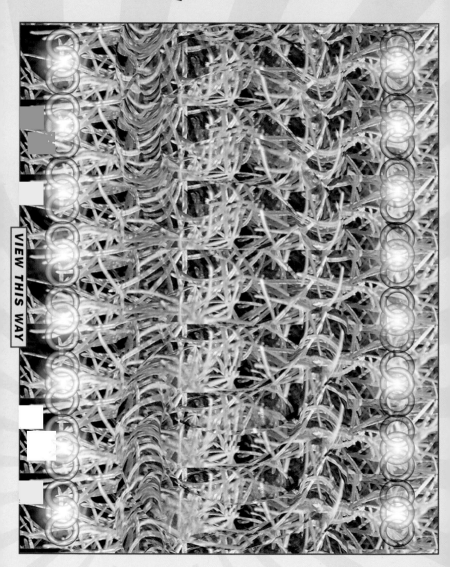

VIEW THIS WAY

38

Eye Tricks

VIEW THIS WAY

Eye Tricks

VIEW THIS WAY

Eye Tricks

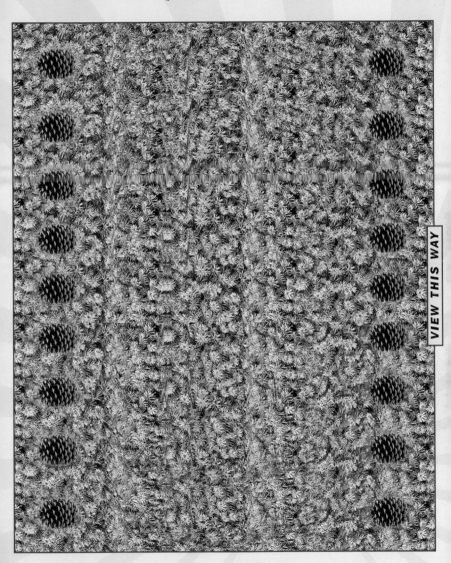

Eye Tricks

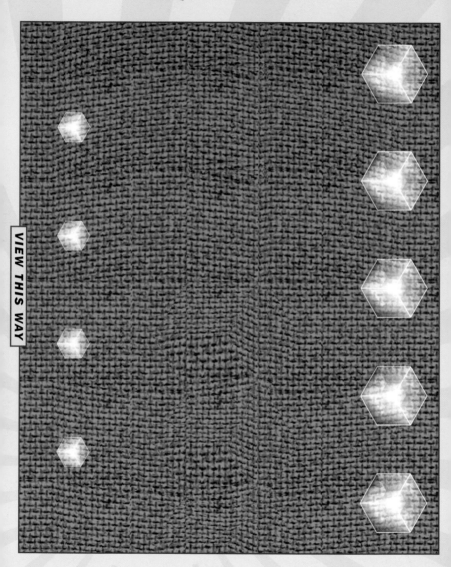

Eye Tricks

VIEW THIS WAY

Eye Tricks

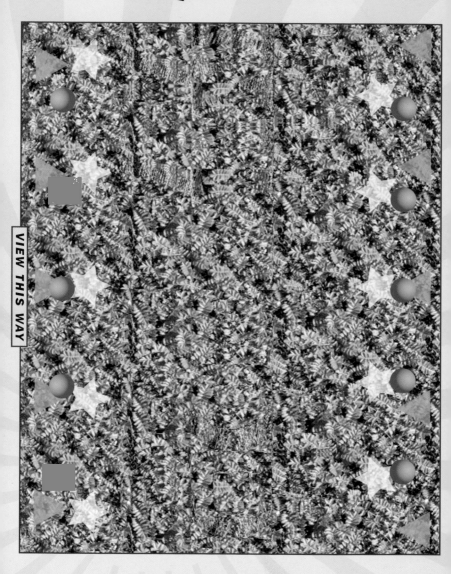

VIEW THIS WAY

44

Eye Tricks

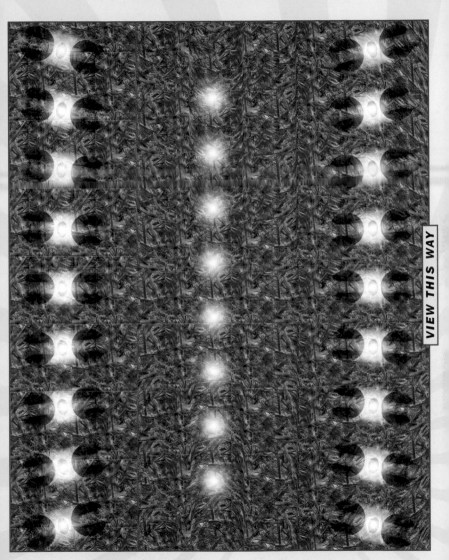

Eye Tricks

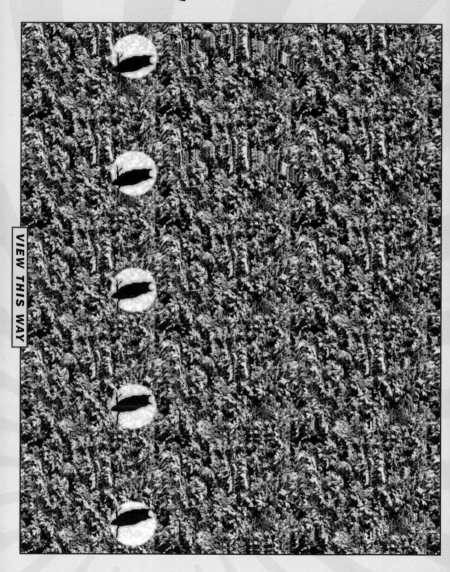

Eye Tricks

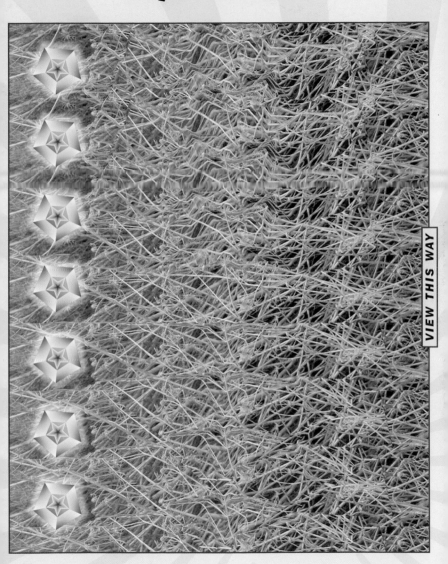

VIEW THIS WAY

Eye Tricks

Eye Tricks

Eye Tricks

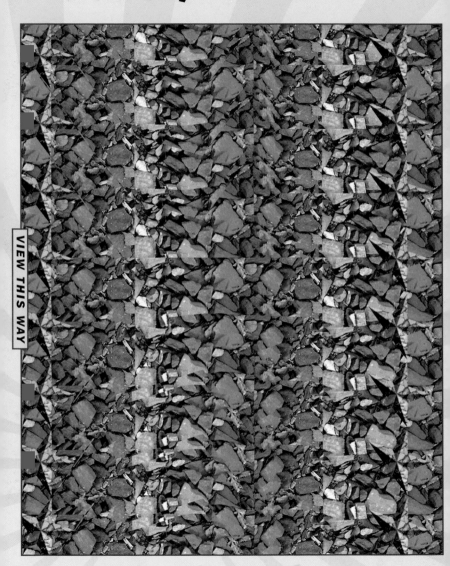

VIEW THIS WAY

Eye Tricks

Eye Tricks

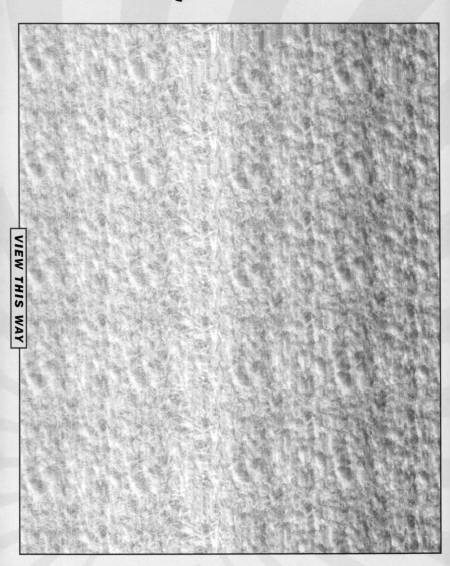

Eye Tricks

VIEW THIS WAY

Eye Tricks

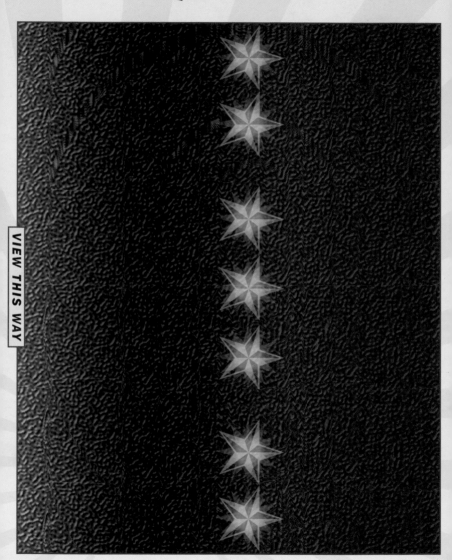

VIEW THIS WAY

Eye Tricks

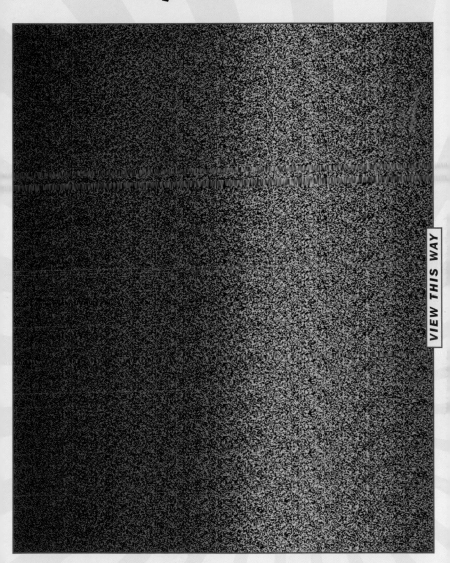

VIEW THIS WAY

VIEW THIS WAY

Eye Tricks

VIEW THIS WAY

Eye Tricks

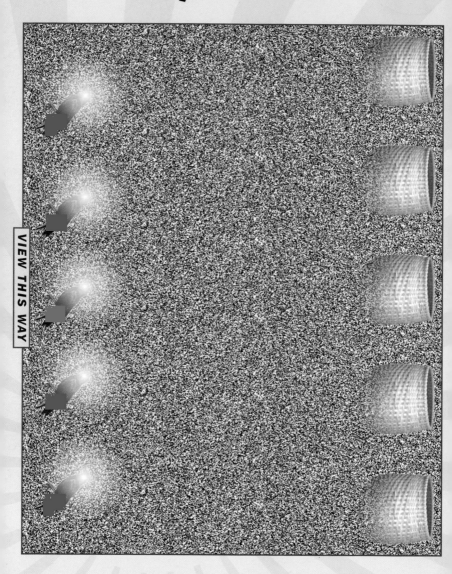

VIEW THIS WAY

Eye Tricks

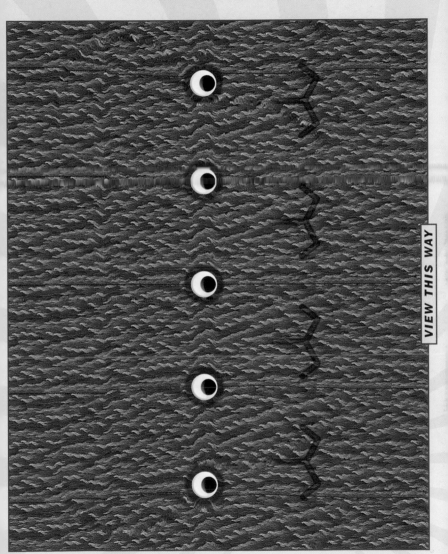

VIEW THIS WAY

59

Eye Tricks

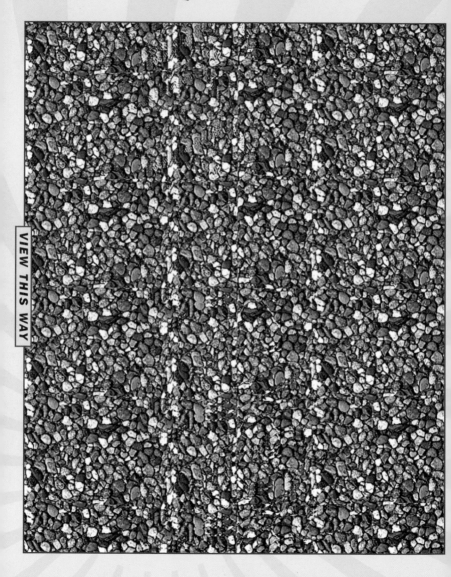

VIEW THIS WAY

Eye Tricks

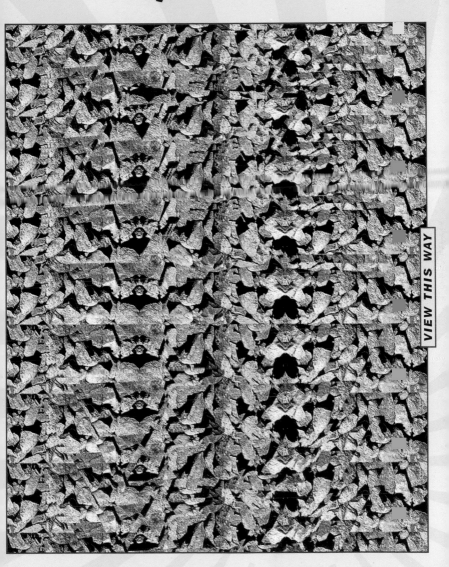

VIEW THIS WAY

Eye Tricks

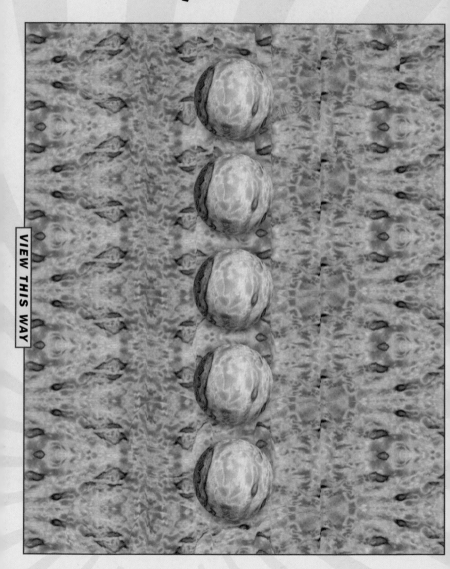

Eye Trick Solutions

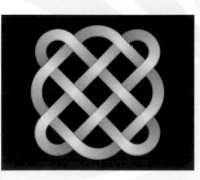

Page 5

Page 6

Eye Trick Solutions

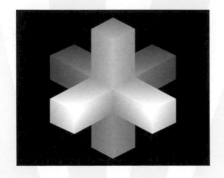

Page 7

Page 8

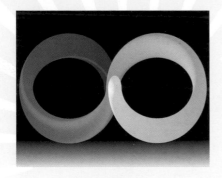

Page 9

Page 10

Eye Trick Solutions

Page 11

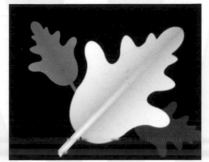

Page 12

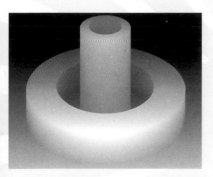

Page 13

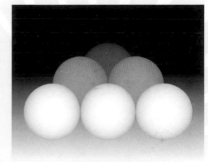

Page 14

Eye Trick Solutions

**Page
15**

**Page
16**

**Page
17**

**Page
18**

Eye Trick Solutions

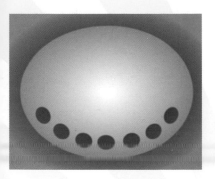

**Page
19**

**Page
20**

**Page
21**

**Page
22**

Eye Trick Solutions

Page 23

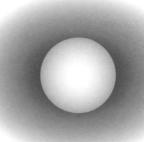

Page 24

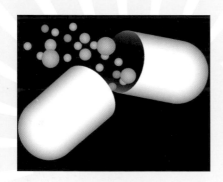

Page 25

Page 26

Eye Trick Solutions

Page 27

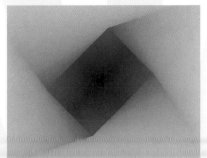

Page 28

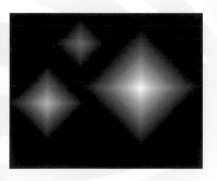

Page 29

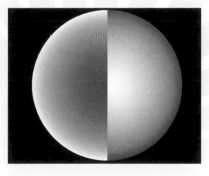

Page 30

Eye Trick Solutions

Page 31

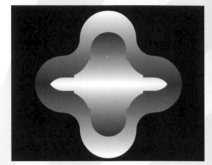

Page 32

Page 33

Page 34

Eye Trick Solutions

Page 35

Page 36

Page 37

Page 38

Eye Trick Solutions

Page 39

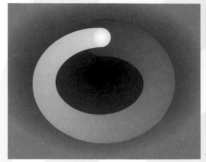

Page 40

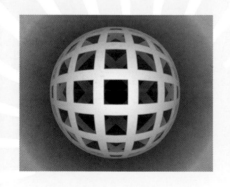

Page 41

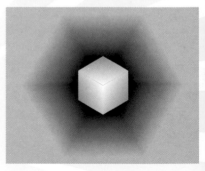

Page 42

Eye Trick Solutions

**Page
43**

**Page
44**

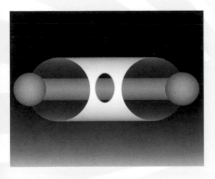

**Page
45**

**Page
46**

Eye Trick Solutions

Page 47

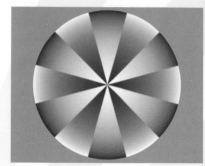

Page 48

Page 49

Page 50

Eye Trick Solutions

Page 51

Page 52

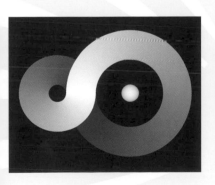

Page 53

Page 54

Eye Trick Solutions

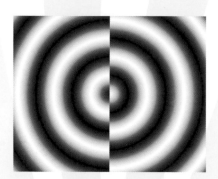

**Page
55**

**Page
56**

**Page
57**

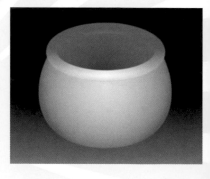

**Page
58**

Eye Trick Solutions

**Page
59**

**Page
60**

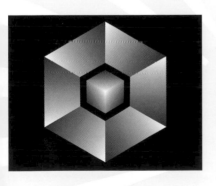

**Page
61**

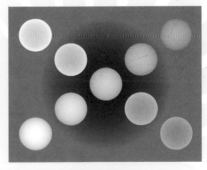

**Page
62**